THE
NEW YORKER
BOOK OF CHRISTMAS CARTOONS

THE
NEW YORKER

RESTORATION HARDWARE
CHRISTMAS

BOOK OF CARTOONS

"'Season's Greetings' looks O.K. to me. Let's run it
by the legal department."

"You're the one who should be 'Time's' Man of the Year."

*"All right. Christmas is over. You can go back to being
your grouchy old self again."*

"They say that every year."

*"It seems ridiculous to get rid of it now,
with Christmas only a couple of months away."*

"Watch who you're calling irrelevant!"

"*Do we have any anti-Christmas cards?*"

"You call that hung by the chimney with care?"

"Oh, and damn it, I nearly forgot! Merry Christmas!"

"We'd love to, Fran, but I'm afraid we'll have to take a rain check.
With us, Christmas is traditionally a family day."

"Miss Harwood, please see to it that the halls are decked."

"Merry Christmas, folks. And I want to say I couldn't be president of this great company without the support of each and every one of you, or people very much like you."

"Yes, I'm somewhat depressed,
but seasonally adjusted I'm probably happy enough."

"Mr. S. Claus, North Pole. Dear Santa:"

"Charles, weren't we happier before we decided to exchange only sensible gifts?"

"We were away over Christmas. How did it go?"

"*Seems to start earlier every year.*"

"The Crandalls wish us a Merry Christmas, and add that they're now worth over two million."

"This one's from you know who, so make a fuss and thank him."

"You have cookie breath again."

"*You haven't been wearing the caftan I gave you for Christmas.*"

*"I wish you a happy holiday, Ed, even though the
leading indicators don't point to it."*

"It's a check for a hundred thousand dollars. Do you like it?"

EDGAR ALLAN POE RETURNS
A CHRISTMAS GIFT

"It's the ghost of that pocketbook I gave you for Christmas."

"It was a nice Christmas—I gave him a dog whistle, he
gave me a police whistle."

"One checker, two packs of cigarettes, two screws, one teapot bird, one piece of coal, three lighters, one Christmas light, one clove of garlic, four boxes of matches, two books, three pieces of broken dish, eggshells, one saltshaker peg, one pen, one cream-cheese wrapper, and one wishbone. All that stuff under the dish cabinet."

"I'm dreaming of a white Christmas."

"Let's not send each other cards this year."

"You smell like a chimney."

"Any discount to the trade?"

"The knees are the first to go."

"No, no, Timmy. Not that one. I'm saving that one for last."

"It's fancy-schmantzy. I just wanted fancy."

"Is it any wonder you got coal in your stocking?"

"Let me refresh your memory. It was the night before Christmas and all through the house not a creature was stirring until you landed a sled, drawn by reindeer, on the plaintiff's home, causing extensive damage to the roof and chimney."

"Lookin' good, Frosty!"

"I think I preferred it _before_ he became an equal-opportunity employer."

"*Darling, trust me. Santa isn't going to give you a network.*"

"I hope that isn't real fur."

THE INCORRECTNESS OF SANTA

Fur

Sack filled with heavily advertised warmongering toys for boys, and saccharine, battery-dependent toys for girls — PLUS TONS OF CANDY

Totally out of shape: bad role model for children

More fur

Leather

 OTHER:

- Doesn't care if elves keel over and die from exhaustion as long as toymaking deadlines are met.
- Overworks his reindeer, too.
- Yet another childhood hero who just _happens_ to be a GUY.

"No, this is crazy. We mustn't."

"Have you been a moral child?"

"Merry Christmas."

"Same to you."

"*Santa Claus is no longer part of my belief system.*"

"Why don't we make it simple this year, and just give everyone the finger?"

"It's Christmas, Melanie. Have young Cosgrove go down to the
street and give something back to the community."

"You can't go wrong with the traditional dead mouse."

"And—what the hell—good will toward women!"

"The charge is driving without a tree."

"I'd like more child support."

"Years ago, there was only one Santa Claus. Now because of genetic engineering, there can be lots of them."

"If you're not a good boy, Santa will bring you only educational toys."

"Things are crazy right now. Let me get back to you after the holidays."

"Nobody move! I think I lost an eye."

"*There is a Santa Claus, but his grandchildren get first pick of all the good stuff.*"

"He knows when you are sleeping. He knows when you're awake."

"*Main floor, aisle six, ladies' scarves. Shopper down.*"

"Another round?"

*"Now, there's a guy who's ruined
Christmas for every other man in the neighborhood."*

THE ST. NICHOLAS DAY MASSACRE

"Get some of the firm's other deadwood and form a carolling group."

SOMETHING NEW FOR THE HOLIDAYS

"Sometimes I don't read my mail."

"Night before Christmas or no night before Christmas, I feel like stirring."

"O.K., we'll meet back here in about five hundred dollars."

"And you must be the domestic partner we refused to extend spousal benefits to."

"*No. 2, please step forward and shake your belly like a bowlful of jelly.*"

"Stop avoiding me. I know when you are sleeping. I know when you're awake."

SANTA'S HELPERS

"My entire family's coming for the holidays."

"*They're especially bold at this time of year.*"

"I'm afraid of it, Barker. It's a little strong, and it could be misinterpreted."

INDEX OF ARTISTS